HILL INC.

Living Free

Cons and other tricks

Wolf Rus

ISBN 978-0-9878741-2-2

FORWORD

I would just like to take this opportunity to say a few quick words. I'd like to start off by saying that I decided to write this book because I am 'retired' from the scam business (as much as I can be) and I wanted to pass on what I learned. I wrote this book some years before I decided to publish it, while I was deep into it. I thought it would be a good time to write my scams and tricks down because everything would still be fresh in my mind. I'd like to say that all the scams I wrote down within the following pages are of my own design. Some are pretty popular and most likely, other people have thought of them in various ways before and some are unique and I am sure that few people have practiced them. I would not have written this book if I thought that an equal book was available on the market already or if I thought that it wasn't worth it. I wanted to show people the real opportunities, which are available out there and also, with which they can protect themselves by knowing what people can do. Whether you are a doer or a seer, I think you will find something of interest to you in this book. I hope you all enjoy, and thank you.

TABLE OF CONTENT

Introduction 1
Rules of the game 2
Keeping your privacy private.. 3
Tips on protecting your goods 4

The Scams

Free CD's, books and more.. 7
Cookies, biscuits and crackers.................................... 12
Get brand new CD's for $5-$10 13
Get a pet dog for free 14
Sperm donation 15
Free '900' phone calls 16
Doubling your money with traveler's cheques 17
Credit cards 19
Home insurance fraud 22
Home insurance fraud part 2 24
Switcharoo.. 25
Free cable.. 26
Clinical testing.. 27
Smaller studies 28
Free movies 29
U.P.S... 30
Bike lock insurance 31
Free newspapers 32
Free newspaper ads.. 33
Free taxi 34
Video game switch 35
Casting jobs... 36
Garbage... 37
Free movies part 2.. 38
Summer camps 39
Mail... 42
Fed-Ex insurance 43
Free payphones... 44

Video stores 45
Courier flights 46
Free credit reports 47
Renting.. 48
Telephones 49
Exchange trick number 2.. 50
Buying and selling 51
Cemeteries 53
NRI and ICS schools.. 54
Lockpicks.. 55
Free PC games 57
Piracy.. 59
Cheques.. 61
Buying and returning 63
Book store buying and exchange.................................. 65
Gambling.. 66
Directory.. 68
Recommended reading.. 72

INTRODUCTION

This should be the last book you'll ever need on small time scams and on how to get stuff for free. The methods have been tried and tested by me and all of which were thought up or refined by me also. I started doing scams in one form or another since I was seven years old. I've tried a lot of things, some worked and some didn't. What you'll find in this book are the ones which did work and have been tested.

This book is partly meant to open your eyes and mind so that you realize that not everything you see is always what it has to be. Every system can be cracked and most have been. Whether it's getting a new identity or just getting into the local gym for free. There's usually always a way around things and maybe by reading this book you'll see things differently and perhaps be able to come up with your own scams.

Performing some or all of the scams in this book can bring in a very, very good income without having to do the dreadful 9-5 rat race. It also gives you the liberty to do it when you want to, on your own time. You can get a whole bunch of stuff for free and you can make a whole bunch of money doing it. Many books on the market claim that you can get a bunch of free things from their tricks but they only disappoint you by giving you rinky-dink tricks like 'free coffee', all you have to do, they tell you, is rent a hotel room for a night and chances are you'll get 'free coffee' in the morning. Personally I think that's brilliant, it's almost as bad as telling you that you can get free rides by asking a buddy to give you a lift. In this book you aren't going to find any tricks on how you can get free salt and pepper by going to a fast food chain and pocketing a few packets of whatever condiment they have available. Here you'll find how you can double your money to make a couple of thousand dollars, how you can get free books or free PC games, along with many others.

I stated a few basic guidelines in the beginning of the book to help you along and then I divided each scam into its own section. I normally gave a brief description of the scam and followed up by going into the details of it and its procedures. I tried my best to make everything as clear as possible so that it wouldn't leave anything unclear. If I say not to do something or to do it a certain way, it's because that's the best way to do it. If you don't follow it exactly you could end up screwing the scam up or screwing yourself up. Finally, in the back of the book you'll find a directory of companies, some of which were mentioned throughout this book. Others I included because they be of some interest to you. With that said, read on and enjoy.

RULES OF THE GAME

There are certain steps you most follow to protect yourself whenever you do anything illegal. These steps are to get the most out of each scam with the least amount of hassles. This is a brief guideline to help you get started and so that you don't run into any difficulties with any of the methods included in the book. The degree to how careful you need to be depends and how much you care about your credit and/or your name.

-First step is mail. Get a mailbox and send all your personal mail there and give a fake address to your mailbox provider. This way your true identity is kept safely tucked away and it makes it harder for anyone to find you.

-Try to never use your name for anything. Pick a different name and use it whenever you need to give your name out, especially for ordering. Depending on how brave you are, generally you won't want to give your real name out.

-Never use the same name for any extended periods of time. This is especially important when ordering through the mail. You could get complications later with credit, or not being able to order from a particular place.

-Never get too friendly with any of the clerks at the post office or any place of the sort. You might end up picking up parcels in many different names from a location so you want to try to be as unremarkable as possible, you don't want to cause any suspicions.

-Never order anything with credit cards to your home address if they are not your credit cards. You don't it to be traceable back to your home if you scammed some credit cards.

-Never order with too many different names at the same time to your home address. You may cause suspicion at the post office and they will launch an investigation as to why you have so many different names going to the same address.

-Follow whatever scam you are doing in this book closely. If I say not to do something or not to skip a step, don't skip it because it must be important if it's in here.

Following these very simple precautions will help you avoid complications further down the line.

KEEPING YOUR PRIVACY PRIVATE

This is a quick lesson on privacy which I will just go over briefly. If you end up doing anything in the slightest way that's illegal and you do it for extended periods of time, it's good to know that no one knows where you live.

The first step you must do is to change your address and get a mailbox (not a P.O. Box). These cost the same as P.O. Boxes and they offer more services. Some companies will not ship or mail anything to postal boxes either. You can find these in almost any city simply by looking in the yellow pages under 'Mail Services' or 'Mail box rental'. These are good because no one knows it's a mailbox. For example, let's say your mail box provider is at 666 Hell's road, Vermont and that your mail box is number 111. Your address would be 666 Hell's road, Apt.111, Vermont. You can substitute the apt. number with a suite number instead. Remember to use a fake address and fake phone number when you go get your mailbox.

Next step is to change your address with all businesses which might have it, credit cards, banks, stores, phone, etc... If you want to be totally private you'll need to disconnect your phone line. You can either reconnect it in a different name; a buddy might be able to use his name to hook a phone up for you. You simply give him the money every month to pay the bill. Second option is to get an answering service from a company in your town. The company gives you a phone number, which you then give out to people and when they call they think you're not home and just leave a message. Disadvantage with this is that you have no phone to make calls with. Alternatively, you can just get yourself a cellular phone, which cost about the same as a regular phone and you have the advantage of being able to take it with you everywhere you go. Same thing can be done with the electricity. You can get a friend to hook it up for you and pay the bills through him.

If you order anything that goes to your home I suggest using a fake name. This includes any sort of deliveries from stores and restaurants. You just need to remember that 'you' don't live there. So you therefore don't let any company know where you live. To them, you live where your mailbox is. And to the mailbox company, you live at the fake address you gave them. This way, if anyone is looking for you, it will make it that much harder to find you. If you are really interested in this subject and want to know exactly how people can find you and how you give yourself away, I recommend finding one of the numerous books on the subject. It will give a much more detail look on how to privatize yourself.

TIPS ON PROTECTING YOUR GOODS

There's nothing worse than arriving home from a weekend and finding your home ransacked and robbed. Even if you have insurance, you've been violated and certain objects cannot be replaced. I'll describe what's good and what's not to keep your home safe. I'll start off by saying that most security alarms are pure garbage. Half the time the alarm will not work and if it does work, the thief can usually bypass it or still rob you blind and be long gone by the time anyone ever gets around to checking your home out.

The first thing you should do is to inspect all the wood frames around the windows and the doors. Most of the time the wood might look in fine condition but with closer inspection you will find that it is rotten through. No matter how many locks you have on a door it won't make a difference if the guy can just push it open due to the rotten wood. Any wood that is rotten should be replaced and if the door and/or windows are the same, they should be replaced too. Most of the time your landlord can replace this for you or if you choose to do it yourself it is fairly inexpensive and easy to do. You should also buy a brass plate that wraps around the door edge where the lock cylinder is. This reinforces the door, which can help you quite a bit. These can be found at almost any hardware store in the same department as the locks. It prevents any one from splitting your door with a crow bar and forcing the lock out.

You will also need a good handle lock along with a couple of deadbolts. Place one of the deadbolts about a quarter of the way up the door and the other a little higher than the door handle, I recommend you do this with all your exterior doors. You can get a door club, which adds a lot of strength to a door, but it needs to be put in place from the inside. So it is only good if you're home or if you choose to put it on your back door only where you know someone might try to get in. The club is a bar, which is put into the floor right behind the door and braces the door (you need to drill a hole in the floor so you can insert it). This prevents any one from kicking your door open while the bar is installed.

If you have any windows, which are accessible from the outside I recommend installing bars on the outside. They're inexpensive and prevent anyone from breaking your window to get in. The cheaper window bars won't do much to prevent anyone from getting if they really want to but chances are it will make them go somewhere else to break in. If the screws to the bars are accessible from the outside, I would suggest that you use screws, which can only be screwed in and not unscrewed. The head of the screw is made a certain way, which makes it near impossible to unscrew it without some alterations to the screw. You can also wedge or brace a piece of wood between the windows and the frame. This makes it impossible to open the window without breaking it.

In some case the outer most window cannot be braced using this method, so you need to fix this or else the thief can just open that window and remove the wood pieces. Place a screw in the frame on top and on the bottom so that they prevent that window from opening. This will solve your problem and remember to use the screws that can only be screwed in. The same method applies to sliding doors; there is always one door (the outer most), which you cannot brace. So you need to use the same trick as the windows.

This pretty much sums it up, following the little preventive measures I just described can save you a lot of trouble if ever that day would come. One final piece of advice is to get a peephole if you don't already have one and to get a baseball bat and keep it near the bed. This way if someone does come to the door, you'll know who it is and if someone does break in, you'll be able to protect yourself.

If someone does break in while you are gone than you need to make sure that that person doesn't find anything that's too interesting. You need to hide your stuff in a place where the thief will not think of looking. There are many places to hide things in, a big bag of flour, a floorboard under, in a hollowed out book in the bookcase, a jar deep in the freezer. Some areas you need to avoid hiding anything in, is the living room and especially the bedroom. That's where most people keep their valuables so it makes it a popular spot for thieves. If you are going to put anything in the bedroom put it in a medium safe, which you can buy at K-mart for under a hundred dollars. Fill half of it with bricks and place a piece of plywood over the bricks and then place your valuables in it in some sort of hard container. This prevents anyone from simply taking off with the safe and in the event where someone would try to take it, having your valuables in a hard container prevents them from being damaged by the bricks.

If you have some bigger items you would like saved and if you are going away for a long period. You can add a fake wall inside one of your closets. You just make a frame using 2x4 pieces of wood, either nailing or screwing the frame into the existing wall and where you want your fake wall to go. Get a piece of drywall, fitted to the proper dimensions and place it in the closet against your 2x4 frame and that's it, you have a new wall. To keep it in place you need to use something which will allow you to remove the wall when you want to. Making four holes, one in each corner of the drywall will allow you to place four big screws, which will go into the wood of the 2x4 frame. You simply unscrew the screws and screw them back when you're done. Make sure that you paint the wall the same color as the rest of the walls in the closet. If there's a light in the closet, I suggest removing it before going away. This will prevent anyone from noticing anything, which might show in better lighting. Hopefully you will never be robbed but if someone does try at least you'll be better off.

THE SCAMS

FREE CD'S, BOOKS
AND MORE

This is probably the best system for getting lots of free stuff and when I say free, I mean totally free with no money required. This little trick is most surely used by a few people but I'm sure very few have developed it to a fine art. You can get CD's, books, office supplies, collectibles, etc... all for free. I'll start by explaining the system and then I will briefly talk about the different things you can get. All of these different companies pretty much use the same system. I'll use the CD clubs as an example but once again, it can be applied to many things.

Start off by getting a membership card, these can be found in magazines or you can ask the company through email or mail to send you one. Once you have a card, fill it out using a fake name, fake phone number but your real address. Some require a signature so just scribble in the name you chose. Next, select the CD's you want, check off the little 'bill me' box and mail the card in. Most of these membership cards already have the postage paid, not that a price of a stamp would kill you.

When you get your parcel through the mail (usually three weeks after you mailed your card), call the company up and change your address, telling them you moved. You will need to give an address that does exist with the right postal or zip code or else it won't register in their computers. By doing this, you take any obligations off your shoulders because the membership is not even in your name. That's all there is to it.

What happens to the unpaid account is pretty simple. For the next year or so the company will send letters every now and then to ask for payment. After which, they will transfer the account to a collection bureau who in turn will write letters of their own also asking for payment. After another year or so, the collection bureau will classify your account as 'unrecoverable' and they'll give up. That is all these companies can really do. They have no power whatsoever, so there is nothing to worry about. Seeing that each of the following sections pertain to each other, I decided to include them all in the same chapter instead of devoting separate chapters to all of these. Some other companies that this relates to are listed in the back of the book.

BOOKS: This has to do with all the book clubs out there and there are a lot of them. There are two varieties to these. The first works exactly as the example I mentioned above except instead of being CD's, they're books. Membership cards for these can be found in TV Guide, history mags, military mags, literature mags, science mags, and other such sources. The way the second type works is very similar except that you need to buy the first book (by sending a money order, it isn't a 'bill me') in order to receive the other three or four books that may be offered.

   Still a pretty sweet deal, four books for the price of one. These clubs are usually found in magazines of the following subjects, woodworking, art, decoration, etc. Overall, the majority of the clubs are 'bill me'.

AUDIO TAPES/PROGRAMS: Once again there are two types of these, the first being from Columbia House Audio book club, which works on the 'bill me' system. They offer various books on tape. The second is from Nightingale Connant and they offer audio programs on topics like self-improvement, business, accelerated learning and so on. For this company you need to call them up to order and when you do, you ask to be billed with the shipment. There is a one hundred dollar credit limit and any order exceeding that amount will have to be paid in advance. You can place different orders with about three or four different names at the same address. I advise calling them up first and asking for a catalogue before doing any ordering. I also advise calling Columbia House Audio Book club, it's very hard to find a card of them in a magazine. The numbers are listed in the back of the book.

CD-ROMS: This is nothing new, Columbia House owns its own club in this as well. They have a pretty good selection of computer games and programs. You get about a hundred and fifty dollars worth of stuff at a cost of ten dollars. You need to fork up ten bucks to get the first selection and with that will come a couple more selections which you selected. They expect you to buy more in the future but all you have to do is to 'move' with your fake name. The cards for this can be found in computer magazines or you can call them or email them and ask for one.

DOLLS: There are a few companies that sell collectible dolls by mail. To find them all you have to do is look in doll magazines and the adverts are plenty in these mags. The best one though would be the Ashton-Drake galleries, which has an extensive catalogue of highly collectible dolls that are extremely easy to sell on the market. They all work in this way, they sell you a doll or many dolls on a payment plan where you make small payments every month. All you have to do is send them the initial down payment; they will send you the doll or dolls. When you get them, your fake person ends up moving and they will never bother you again. The trick is to look for dolls that are worth a lot and that have long payment plans, such as an eight-month plan. The more payments you are supposed to make, the cheaper the doll is. You can usually order several dolls at once and have several names living at the same address. You can gather a collection of a dozen dolls or so and then sell it in the paper or on the net. It works quite well.

COLLECTIBLE PLATES: There's basically only one plate company that has a 'bill me' option and that company would be the Bradford Exchange. It's known all around the world as being the main marketplace for plates. Most of them sell for thirty or forty dollars but they can go up in value so they are easy to sell. You will have to look for plate offers in magazines, TV guides, or you can call them up and ask for a catalogue. It's a 'bill me' so it's the same system.

You can order two plates per name and can usually have a few names per address. The other plate companies ask to be paid in advance before they ship anything, so they are of no worth to us.

CD'S: I mentioned CD's in my example so I will only elaborate a little on CD's. Columbia house is the main club and they offer about twelve or thirteen CD's per membership. BMG will usually give you six or seven CD's at a time and CDHQ will give you the same offer as BMG. All of them work the same way, basically two memberships per address, when you get the CD's you call them up and change your address and keep repeating. Keep in mind that CDHQ is owned by Columbia House and therefore, can only have two memberships at a time from the both of them combined. If you plan on getting audio books from Columbia also, you might end up not getting everything.

FRANKLIN MINT: The Franklin Mint is the world's largest privately owned mint, what that means, I don't know but they are. This company is a really good one to get stuff from because they have a very extensive catalogue of jewelry, swords, collectibles, etc. The way this works is very similar to the dolls, they allow you to buy something on payment plans and most items are payable in ten months which really brings down the amount of money you need to spend. When I first started this, their credit limit was around the two thousand dollar mark. Now it's around a thousand dollars, if you order anything over that, they will want a credit check done on you before they ship anything out. So what this means is that for around ninety bucks or so, they will send you something that's worth around a thousand dollars with only a fake signature. Change your address when you receive your merchandise, just like the other ones. You're allowed quite a few different names per address but you can only make one order per name.

Most of the things they sell can easily be sold at half their value from the catalogue; jewelry can be sold privately for about a third of the value because they overprice their jewelry. If you want to get things to sell I recommend ordering their deluxe editions of popular board games such as scrabble, monopoly, Chinese checkers and so on. These sell for about seven hundred dollars; you get it for seventy bucks or so and end up selling it for around four hundred. Good profit. When you order their catalogue make sure that you ask which catalogues are available as they have different ones that come out throughout the year that specialize in certain collectibles. Also, they have a thirty-day money back guarantee. So if you can't sell something you can send it back and get something different.

MAGAZINES: It's very simple to get most of the magazines on the market for free every month. This is also a good way of gathering ordering cards from the various 'bill me' clubs. All you need to do is go to a big magazine store and take a look at all the magazines you would like to have. Take a look at the subscription card inside the magazines and if it's marked 'bill me' then you can order the magazine free of charge.

You place the subscription card in your pocket or if you plan on taking a lot of cards, you can place them all in one magazine and buy it. The rest is pretty self-explanatory but I will state a few points. Use fake names for all of these, and when you do start receiving a magazine subscription, it will only last a few months before they stop sending magazines due to the fact that you didn't pay them. If you want to get a magazine coming in continuously you need to send a new subscription card every two months. And every three months you call and cancel the old subscription.

There are quite a few other minor companies that have similar systems and products. Anything that has a 'bill me' on it is good to go, it's actually code for 'free' but not everyone sees that. I think that all the information I provided above is sufficient knowledge to help you find new and interesting companies to order from. Using the 'bill me' scams above to the maximum efficiency can give you a very comfortable living every month. I should also like to state that most companies only accept two orders per address unless otherwise noted above. If you are ordering things to make money and not to keep for yourself, then you could do the following. When you receive your package, wait for the bill to come by mail and when it does call the company up. Tell them you never received your package and you are still waiting for it. They will reship your order out again. When you get the second order that is when you call them up and change your address. This way you double your orders and get more stuff to sell. This works with all companies because none of the parcels require your signature.

COOKIES, BISCUITS
AND
CRACKERS

All it takes is a quick phone call and you'll get a few free boxes and coupons delivered to your door. Buy a box of cookies from a major brand name and enjoy a few of them, after which you call the customer service number on the side of the box. Tell them that there was a tiny green worm about half an inch long on one of the cookies. Remember that you are calling to complain, so tell them that you are disappointed in their product and so on but don't be rude on the phone or else you'll get nowhere. They might ask you if you still have the worm and/or cookie in which case you tell them you were absolutely disgusted with it that you stepped on it and/or threw it out. They'll take your address down and depending on which company you're dealing with, they'll send you coupons by mail or send a deliveryman with a variety of product. That's all there is to it and you can do this with all sorts of different companies and products.

BRAND NEW CD'S
FOR $5-$10

This lets you return used CD's to a music store and a get a new one of whatever you choose in exchange. Go to a used music store or pawnshop and look at their selection of CD's. You'll find that most of these range from five to ten dollars and can go for as little as a couple of dollars. It doesn't matter what you buy, just make sure that it is available from a major music store like HMV and make sure that the CD's are in mint condition. You can usually do this with two or three CD's at a time. Now you go to the new music store (HMV, Virgin, whichever), buy the same CD's you bought at the used music store. You then go back with the used ones and the bill and say that you don't like them and get your money back. Return on a different occasion with the new CD's you bought (not opened of course) and say that they were a gift (hence, no receipt) and you don't like them and would like to get something else. They will let you get whatever you want in the store for the equivalent value of the CD's you brought back. This trick is good is good if you want to get those hard to find CD's not available anywhere else except at a major retail store.

GET A PET DOG
FOR FREE

If you're looking for some company and want a pet then you should have no problems getting a dog for free from the SPCA. Normally you need to pay a sizeable fee if you get a dog from the SPCA but using this trick will get you one for free. Go to the local SPCA and say that you want to volunteer your services. There are many different functions at the SPCA that someone can do. Depending on the SPCA you'll start off by doing cleaning chores and walking dogs. When you fill out an application form put a fake address and name, as for the phone number, you tell them that you recently moved and that your phone line is not connected yet. Tell them that you will call them whenever they want to see if you will be needed. They don't normally ask for ID but if they do, tell them that you don't have your wallet on you and you will bring it by next time you come in. When you do show up next time, you of course, forgot it again.

When you start volunteering your services, you will usually be walking several dogs at the same time. Simply walk a couple of blocks or so to the nearest payphone. Tie the leashes beside the pay phone and call the SPCA and tell them that there are several dogs tied and that they should take a look at it. Keep the dog you want with you and make sure that the SPCA picks up the dogs before you go home. Once you're home you'll have a new friend to keep you company. This trick may not work in small towns because they will probably not need volunteers as often as the shelters in larger cities. It works out good on both ends, both for the dog and for you. The dog gets a home and you don't have to spend a lot of money for a pet. On a side note, do take care of the dog. It was in a shelter for a reason and it needs a better home then the previous.

SPERM DONATION

This one system won't make you work too hard I'm sure and of course, is available to men only. The way to locate sperm banks is to look in the yellow pages under 'medical clinics'; from there you'll have to look for a sperm bank. If none are listed look under the same heading for female fertility clinics. Chances are the fertility clinic will be taking donors or they will know where one can go to make such a donation. Once you find them, call them and ask them if they are accepting sperm donors at the time. If so, ask to make an appointment to donate sperm. You'll basically go in, give a sample in a jar and wait for the results.

They will mainly check your sperm count the first time to see if it is up to par. If you are having a lot of sex your count may be down so I suggest that you make like a monk and seclude yourself prior to going in the first time, in order to raise your count. If your sperm is good, you will then be ask to come back in to do some blood tests and to speak with a doctor. If everything checks out you will then be paid every time you go in to donate. The average is around thirty-forty dollars a shot and there will also be a limit as to how many times you can donate, usually once or twice a week is the maximum. There's usually some nice reading material and everything is kept very hush, hush.

FREE 900 PHONE CALLS
FOR A MONTH

This is really quick and simple and doesn't take much time on your part. There's a way of getting a full free month of access to 900 numbers from your telephone company. Just make all the calls you want up to a couple of hundred dollars worth in the span of a few weeks shortly after your previous phone bill. Make sure that you call the same number all the time. When you get your phone bill for that month, call the telephone company and complain about your bill, saying that you're outraged and that you never made those phone calls. They will then give you a 'grace month' and take the 900 charges off your phone bill.

DOUBLING YOUR MONEY
WITH
TRAVELER'S CHECKS

This trick doesn't require a lot of hard work but it does require plenty of planning and some cash up front. You'll enjoy this one because it's fun, easy, and you get to travel. If you don't have a lot of cash on hand then I would suggest that you wait until you do have money because you only get to do this a couple of times. Try to get as much cash for this scam as you can, the more you have to start out with, the more you'll make in the end.

The way this scam works is as follows; you buy travelers checks, travel somewhere, and then report them lost or stolen so that you can get your checks back. The most you should claim is about twenty-five hundred dollars; anything over and you will have to wait a while to get your money back. I suggest not claiming anything over fifteen hundred dollars, the more money you claim, the further away from home you need to be. For fifteen hundred you should be across the continent or in a different country.

The first thing you need to do is get your money together and go buy travelers checks. You have a few companies to choose from such as American Express, Visa, Thomas Cook, Citibank, and MasterCard. I recommend Amex as they are pretty easy going and ask very little questions. Buy your checks a good two weeks in advance prior to your trip and get them mainly in fifties and hundreds, remember that everything you do needs to look as if you are planning a real trip. Don't buy your checks the day before you leave and claim them stolen the day after because it will look suspicious. You'll also need to pick a destination like a very touristy area. Once you've taking care of this it'll be time to leave. Note that if you are traveling across the United States, you could travel by Greyhound, which is extremely cheap. If you claiming a large sum, you should plan on being away for a week, less if you're claiming less.

Once you're at your destination you should get comfortable and spend about a third of your checks legitimately to show that you really are on vacation. You should cash a couple at a bank, this way the money goes straight into your pocket and you don't need to buy anything. After being there long enough and spending enough of the checks, it'll be time to set the plan in action. You'll have to spend the rest of your checks within a half hour or so. There are a couple of ways to do this; one is to buy small items at many different stores with a separate check for each store. The other is to buy a few large items at several stores and then bring them back afterwards with the receipt and get your money back. Once you've completed this the dirty work is done. I should mention something here about signing your name, if you're alone I would suggest that you learn to sign with your opposite hand prior to leaving.

When you spend your 'stolen' checks you would then sign with your opposite hand or sign a little differently with your proper hand. If you are with a friend then you should get your friends to cash your checks for you. You might also have to show ID when you cash your checks, depending on where you are. If this is so then use cards with no photos on them. Most merchants just want to get your money and won't bother asking for any ID whatsoever.

Wait a few hours and then make a phone call to the police station. When you call them up tell them that you lost your camera case or that someone stole it when you were at a restaurant and tell them that your wallet was in it along with the traveler's checks. They will ask you basic questions such as where you lost it and what did you have it in and so on. They might ask you to go down to the police station to file a report in person. After you've called the cops, make a call to the traveler's checks company and tell them what happened. It's all pretty simple but make sure that you have a passport and birth certificate on your person because you will need ID to get your checks back. You will probably need to tell them your social security number (remember that this card is in your wallet, which is stolen) so pretend that you have it memorized. They will also ask for the police report number so just call back the police station and ask for it. Once all the calls have been made they will tell you where to go to get your new checks, it's all usually done in one day. When you get your checks back you can do whatever you want.

There's no danger of getting caught but just make sure you don't skip any steps because if you do they might deny your claim and you'll have to wait several weeks to get your money back that was 'stolen'. Remember that they have a guarantee of refunding lost or stolen travelers checks with no hassles and that you are the victim here.

CREDIT CARDS

Here's another scam that can give you lots of money if you sell the merchandise that you get from the credit cards. This is illegal of course but if it's done on a small scale and if you follow my directions you won't get caught and it's failsafe. It goes like this; first you'll need credit card numbers before you do anything else. There's several ways to get them, the most common method is as follows. Store dumpsters are a great source of numbers. Go to the dumpsters in the back of large stores or gas stations or almost any business that would see a lot of credit card transactions. You'll be looking for bags with papers in them, once you've found that, you'll need to search for sale slips that have credit card numbers on them. In other words, sales which were made with credit cards. Businesses are not really allowed to throw these out but they always do, usually photocopies of sales slips always end up in the trash. What's good about finding sale slips is that you also have the expiration date of the credit card written on it. This is the method I prefer.

When you have your numbers you then proceed to get a few magazines of subject matters which interest you and order catalogues from different companies you would like to purchase from. In the meantime while you're waiting for those to come in you will need to verify the numbers. Look for 900 sex lines and find ones that take credit cards and that have a 1-800 number for card users. Make sure that it is automated when you call. The only drawback to these is that they don't verify expiration dates; this is bad only if you have a card and you don't know what the expiration is.

The next step before ordering is to find a place to get your stuff shipped to. You'll need to find an empty apartment or business, such as a warehouse that is not occupied but that isn't too obvious that there is no one there. You can even send it to your neighbor's house if you know they are not home during the day. One other option is to rent a really cheap apartment by the month just to receive your packages and once your stuff comes in you ditch the place. Make sure you rent under a fake name. When you've completed the above requirements you'll be ready to order from your catalogues. When you order, call only 1-800 numbers and order only from places that ship by UPS. No UPS, no order. Before you go wild and order anything from anywhere, it is wise to write down everything that you order in a little book, along with when you expect it to arrive, how much it cost, what company it is and under what name it is coming in. Use the following guidelines to help you order.
-Make purchases of a couple of hundred dollars from each place and make a couple of bigger purchases.

-Order items that are easy to sell like camera equipment, paintball guns, silver bars, etc.

-Don't order a bunch of knick-knacks unless you plan on keeping them because they will be useless to sell.

-Order from about a dozen places or so for each credit card.

-If you don't know the cards expiration date order from at least twenty different places, changing the expiration date every time you order.

-If using a card with the name that is obviously of the opposite sex, simply say that you are using your wife/husbands card.

-Block your number with *67 or the equivalent and if you can't do that then order from a payphone (making sure it's quiet and private). Many businesses have call display and they'll write your number down and may actually call you if there is something wrong with the card.

-Give them your drop-off address and a fake phone number and if they ask, "Is this the billing address of the card?" you say, "Yes."

-Never call the company back to see how your order is coming along. If you plan on ordering from that company again, make sure that you wait a couple of months and that you use a different address.

-Even though there seems to be a lot of security involved with credit cards, there really isn't. Most companies don't care, and many mistakes make it through the system.

Once you've finished all your ordering it will now be time to wait for your parcels to arrive. When you order they will tell you around how much time it will take for shipping. And when you think you will be getting parcels, it will be time for you to start checking the address you gave. I advise to check once in the early afternoon and again around four or five PM. Check your address out for a good two weeks after you've ordered to make sure that you don't miss anything. If you are renting a place to receive your parcel then you can wait at the place. The Ups guy will leave a yellow delivery slip on the door or mailbox and will usually attempt another delivery the next business day. All you do now is sign the slip with the person's name (credit card), leave instructions for the UPS man, and put the slip back where he left it. When he comes back, he will take the slip and leave the parcel on the doorstep. If it looks like an unsafe place to leave a parcel, the deliveryman may not leave it but it depends on the driver. The reason I said not to get anything ship by mail is because if you are not there to receive the package, you will need to go pick it up at the post office and you will need to show ID. And it usually takes longer to receive packages by mail then it does by UPS.

When all the parcels have arrived, it will now be time to throw away any records you've kept, along with any receipts from the packages or any other paperwork. And throw them away in a safe garbage can. I normally sell all the stuff I get either in the paper or on the Internet.

To conclude, I need to say that the person you used the credit card from will not have to pay for what you ordered. At most, they will pay a small insurance fee from the card company and all purchases will be wiped from their account. No investigation will be made, especially if you keep it on a small scale. Just don't order with fifteen different credit cards at the same address. Remember that if any scam is done on a small scale, it will not be dangerous.

This is one of my favorite systems and no one really gets hurt. I love this because it's like Christmas every time you order. You never know what is going to come in and what isn't. Not to mention that you can make some very good money with this. When you don't think you'll be receiving anything else at the address, stop going there and don't go there again. You can then wait a few months and start ordering again at a different location and do the same thing. If anything is caught either by the credit card company or by the store, they'll simply cancel the order and you won't get anything. The credit company will only notice a pattern when you start placing orders with ten or twenty different names from their company. If this happens, they will then proceed to investigate the matter to find out who is doing all this. It's all about not being greedy, always keep that in mind.

HOME INSURANCE
FRAUD

This is a big one so if you're going to do this, you must make sure that you follow every step described. The basic idea of this is to get insurance for your home or apartment (if you don't already have it) and then at a later date you report a robbery and make a claim with the insurance company. The first step is to go out and get insured. Call the major companies for pricing and pick one that you like. Only make sure that you get insurance from a big name insurance company. Don't take a chance with smaller companies as they might screw you. Get a policy of around fifteen thousand dollars and make sure that your policy will replace merchandise at the full market value. Also read the entire policy or contract to see what their criteria are for claims.

Once you have completed this, you'll now have to wait around five or six months before you make your claim. I know this is a long time but the benefits are quite worthwhile. During this waiting period you should start gathering any and all receipts you can get your hands on. Also, take pictures of items that are worth any money. These are almost as good as receipts. Even manuals and instruction books are good. To add an extra touch, though this is absolutely not necessary but it's better being safe than sorry, go to a police station and ask to have an engrave to mark your possessions, they will usually rent them out. Keep in mind also that you don't actually need to engrave anything. Mark the back of any pictures and receipts with the serial numbers and also model number, if any.

The next step is to get robbed when the time has come. If you are claiming anything that is in your home you should get them out a couple of weeks before. Remember that thieves today do in-and-out jobs. They don't come in with a moving truck and empty your entire apartment out. So keep this in mind, the things you claim should all fit in a car and they should all be easy things to carry and of value. Camera equipment, computer, VCR, DVD, game systems like X-box, bicycle, so on are good items to claim.

You will need to figure out an entry point from which the thieves will come in. It will have to be a forced entry such as a front door or a window. For windows, most thieves use a screwdriver or a crowbar to pry the window open. For doors, either a crowbar to split the frame or just a good kick usually works. Either way, you will need to do this yourself and do it when you come back from out of town. It's good to go somewhere for the weekend with someone and when you come you can call the cops to report the burglary. If you have a friend that could do this for you while you are out of town it would be good. Remember to mess up the place a little bit before the cops come. When they do come to your house, just act normally as if you really did get burgled.

Give the cops your story and they'll ask you some basic questions, do you know anyone that would do this and where you were during the time of the incident and a few other questions like that. They'll ask the neighbors some questions too like if they heard anything or saw anything. Before leaving they'll give you some claim forms to fill out of what was stolen. Call the insurance company the next day to let them know you got robbed. Fill out the forms as to what is missing. Note that you don't need to have proof of everything that was stolen. If you don't have proof that you owned something, the insurance company will give you the market value of what the item is worth used. Once you've filled out the police forms, bring them to the police station to hand them in and ask for copies. The insurance company will send an agent over to talk to you and to take a look at the burglary. It's just a formality and the agent will take the list you made for the police also.

It is good at this point to give the agent any receipts of any items you had, and also any instruction booklet or manual, anything that proves you had the item. This way you'll get more money for your goods. Anything that is on the list that you don't have proof that you owned it, you will receive a fraction of what it's worth. Unless of course, you go to the store and buy the same item, which got stolen, in which case they will give you full value. When the settlement comes, ask for a rundown of all the items and how much you are getting for each of them. For any items which you have no proof of ownership, tell them that you will buy the item to replace it. You then send them a copy of the receipt of the item or items and they send you a check for the difference. As I mentioned before, make sure that you get a policy that will refund you the full value of the items you lost or else you won't get the above option and you'll get less money. If you buy anything in order to get a receipt to send to the company, remember that you can simply bring the item back to the store and get your money back. Because you still have the original receipt and you've satisfied to requirements of the insurance company. This is a great system and it works perfectly but read this over and over again if you plan on doing this.

HOME INSURANCE FRAUD
PART 2

This is a continuation of the first part. It's for people that aren't up to doing the 'big one'. Follow the same procedures as part one, all the way up to the point of getting robbed. Instead of robbing your home, you'll rob yourself outside of your home. Make sure that the policy you get or have has coverage outside of your home. Most will give you about ten percent of what your policy is worth. So if you are insured for ten thousand, you'll be covered for one thousand dollars outside the home.

The best item for this is a bike or a camcorder or camera, anything along those lines. When the time comes, call the cops and tell them what happened. Like, you locked up your bike went in the store and came out an hour later to find that your bike was missing. Of course you never actually brought your bike there. Another way to go is to tell them that you fell asleep on the bus and woke up to find your camera missing. Whatever you like that is believable. Once you called the cops, you then call the insurance company to let them know of your situation. This one little trick is simpler than the first one and works quite well. You also have a wide range of scenarios to choose from, anything from skis to card collections.

SWITCHAROO

This little beauty allows you to buy something at a big store and then bring it back to get your money back while still keeping the item you originally purchased. How is this possible? Simple, here's how it's done. Go to a big store (which doesn't have surveillance cameras) and buy something that you like and that also fits in the stores shopping bags so don't buy anything too big and don't buy anything that is behind a lock and key.

Once you bought what you wanted, you go home and wait a few days. Go back to the store with the receipt and the stores shopping bag folded up in your pocket. Get the same exact item that you bought off the shelf, walk around the store for a while and make like you're shopping. Finally, take the bag out of your pocket and go to the customer's service desk. It's good to do this when there are a lot of people waiting in line at the desk. When you get to the counter, you place the item on it and put the bag beside it along with the receipt. Now you simply say that you are returning this and want your money back. That's all there is to it and you got something for free. Remember to find out the stores return policy, these signs are usually located at the cash or near the exits.

FREE CABLE

This trick is so obvious that most of you probably thought of this but I thought it worthwhile enough to include it. You need live in apartment building in order to do this effectively. Look for a cable running to someone else's apartment outside your windows and doors or almost anywhere outside your building, which can be reached. If you find one than you are in luck and may be getting cable TV quite soon.

Next you need to go to the hardware or electronics store and buy some supplies. You'll need enough cable to run from the cable outside to your TV set. You'll also need two TV cable screws, fastening brackets to attach the cable to the wall and a cable splitter/adapter. You wait until it is quite late at night to do this and until you think that your neighbors are sleeping then you go out and do the deed. The reason for this is that you are going to disconnect the cable for a few minutes so it wouldn't be good if they would be watching TV while you were doing this. Cut the cable and install the cable screws on either end. Screw them into the adapter and screw your cable into it as well. You'll need to secure your cable to the wall, all the way to your window so that it looks very neat. What you can do is cut the cable again just outside your window and repeat the steps above. This way you can connect your cable to your TV only when you are watching it. Make sure that the reception is clear and coming in just fine, because if it's not, chances are that it's not coming in clear on the guys TV you stole cable from too. So he might call the company to complain about the reception and they'll send a cable guy over to check it out.

CLINICAL TESTING

This is a great way of getting money very easily and very legally. There are many clinics out there that are looking for people to be guinea pigs for them so that they could test various drugs. Most of the drugs that are tested in these places are drugs that have been around for a long time or common drugs, which are coming onto the market under a new brand name. Most of them are far from being dangerous and you get to choose if it's to your liking or not. They let you know of any side effects (if any) that you might have. And if you freak out while you're there, all clinics let you leave at any time. You of course forfeit your pay.

The pay is good, you get fed and there are various entertainment facilities to keep you occupied while you stay there. Stays can last from a few hours to a month, even longer. Finding these clinics is fairly easy. Look in the newspapers in the employment section. You can also look in the yellow pages under 'clinical testing' or 'drug research'. Call them up and ask them if they are doing any studies and/or taking any volunteers. If they are, they will ask you to come in for a medical exam to see if you are a good candidate. If you're clean then you have nothing to worry about but if you smoke (if they ask for non-smokers) or did any sort of drugs shortly before going to the clinic you might not make it through for testing. To get around this, you could do the study with a 'clean' friend and let him do your urine samples. Most studies pay from a hundred dollars to many, many thousands of dollars.

This is also a good way to getting a free medical done on you. You can simply go in for the initial testing to get a basic checkup. Or if you decide to do the whole study, you'll come out of it with a complete medical including, cholesterol level, blood cell counts, blood work, etc.

SMALLER STUDIES

These are small studies conducted by universities and most of them are very tame. They usually involve anything from drinking beer and testing your reaction afterwards to having brain imaging done on you with minor radiation. The pay is not that great but it is money.

You can find these in the 'help wanted' section of your local newspaper or you can check out the billboards on the campus of the university. Some studies ask for specific people, such as someone with a history of depression or of alcohol abuse or anything like that. If you need the money, remember you can lie about everything and pretend that you do have a history of whatever they are looking for. I've done quite a few of these smaller studies but I only did them to get extra cash when I wasn't doing anything else. Because I find that for the amount of money you get paid for these, it isn't really worth it unless you are absolutely not doing anything else. Money is money and everyone can use a little more and these smaller studies are good if you are afraid of doing the bigger studies.

FREE MOVIES

This is the way to go to most of the movie premieres for nothing except a little footwork. By the way, I should mention this really only works in big cities. Look in the local city newspapers; usually the free community papers are better. A lot of times there will be tickets advertised in the paper and all you have to do is show up at a certain time, at a certain store to pick them up. There are a limited number of tickets available so it's best to be there a little before you are supposed to be there. First come, first serve. If you don't see anything the first time you look, keep looking. Look at that paper whenever it comes out and you'll get your chance.

Another way is if you are a group of people going to the movies. All you need is to have two people buy their tickets; everyone splits the cost of the two tickets and everyone gets in. Here's how it actually works. Two people go in the theater with the tickets, one comes out with the two ticket stubs. Gives one of the stubs to the buddy and they both go back in. You keep repeating this until everyone is in the theater. It's very simple and idiot proof.

U.P.S.

This trick saves the parcel fee UPS might charge when you receive a delivery such as a COD order you place or an international package you ordered, where you would have to pay for customs and taxes.

When they deliver your package the first time you don't answer the door. They will leave a yellow slip saying they tried to deliver but no one was home and they will also write down the amount you owe them. At this point you need a blank check. This can be had at a lot of banks for free and they are totally blank, no account number, no name, etc. Another source is if you have a credit card. A lot of cards now have checks you can write out using your card number. These are also good because they are totally blank also. Basically, you write out the check to UPS for the amount they stated. Write in a fake name, fake account number and so on. It doesn't matter if the name on the parcel doesn't match up with the name on the check. On the yellow slip, you state that you give permission to the driver to leave the parcel at the door and you also write that the check is in an envelope in the mailbox. Next day, the UPS guy will come and take the slip and the check and leave the parcel at the door.

That's it. All they do when the check bounces is write you several letters stating that you owe them money. It will be in the fake person's name because that's the name written on the check. You can simply call UPS and tell them that that person doesn't live there anymore and you give them a forwarding address.

BIKE LOCK INSURANCE

This scam will get you around one thousand dollars or so but it's imperative that you follow everything outlined. This is so you don't run into problems. The first thing that you'll have to do is to go out and buy a U-lock as soon as possible. You need to purchase one that has an insurance policy with it and it should be for at least one thousand dollars. This system works like this. You buy a lock, wait a month or so then report the bike stolen and claim the insurance money. If the lock has an insurance policy of a thousand dollars then you'll be covered for anything up to that amount.

Purchase the lock from a big department store because it's easier to return. Once you buy the lock, make a photocopy of the receipt and of the form that you need to fill out. Fill the form out and mail it in right away. You will need to give some information about your bike so make sure you have a bike in mind. You'll need to write down a serial number, you can take this off a bike at a store, just make sure it matches the model of the bike that's going to get stolen. Also, at this time, go to a bike store and tell them that such and such a bike was stolen and that you need a receipt or an evaluation of the particular bike you had in order to get the full value from the insurance company. If you tell them that you are going to come back when you get your money and buy the bike again, most stores will give you a receipt. In the meantime while you are waiting for the right time to do the scam. Bring your lock back to the store and get your money back for it.

When the time comes you call the cops and report your bike stolen. After that you call the lock company and tell them what happened. The story is that you locked your bike somewhere and when you got back the bike and lock was gone. Or you can say you found the lock if you can pry it open at home and then you can just pretend it was left behind, though you won't be able to get the money back for the lock. Once they have all the information they need they will process your claim and you should get a check within a month.

FREE NEWSPAPERS

Find a newspaper that allows you to be billed by mail instead of having a collection boy pick up the money. Most major newspapers work like this these days. To find out if a certain paper does bill you like that simply call them up and ask what sort of payment and billing options they have. Give a fake name when you call and have it delivered to your home. When it stops being delivered because of non-payment, call them up and change the address. You can then start having it delivered again under a different name. It's very simple and very straightforward and you should not have any problems.

FREE NEWPAPER ADS

It's pretty much the same principle as the previous scam. You need to find a newspaper that lets you be billed for placing ads. Not all of them will do this but there are some. When you've done this you then call them up and say that you would like to place an ad. Give them a fake number, fake name and fake address. You tell them the ad that you would like to place and you give them your real phone number in the ad so this way, the account has a fake number but your ad has the real one. It's as simple as that and you don't have to do anything more but just let your ad run.

FREE TAXI

You can get free cab rides if you know how. You basically ditch the cab, but you do it with a little more style then just running out of the cab at a stoplight. Beforehand you will need to know or find out a building that has a front entrance and a rear exit, which you can access. An apartment building will usually have this even some restaurants or bars. You should try to find a place that is either near your home or near a place where you would normally take a cab. Once you've got a place scoped out, keep it in mind. When you're in need of a cab ride and can't afford one, call one anyways and use this trick.

You tell the driver that your destination is further than the actual place you will be getting off. About halfway say that you need to stop by to either pick up something or pick up someone or that you need to drop something off. The driver at this point might ask you to leave some sort of deposit. If that's the case, make sure that you don't have more than a couple of dollars in your wallet and that you'll pay him with money you have at your final destination. Make it a point that you are in a hurry and have no time to argue. You go in the marked building, and hurry to the rear and make a quick getaway. The cab drive will wait five minutes or so before he goes in to look for you. By then you'll be long gone and remember that if you plan on doing this more than once, use different cab companies.

VIDEO GAME SWITCH

If you play any gaming system that utilizes cartridges instead of CD's then you'll appreciate this trick. This works with Nintendo game cartridges, Game boy, and any other system with cartridges. You can either do this with games that you don't play anymore or you can find a store that is liquidating selected games. Usually these are the games that don't sell. It doesn't matter what game you buy, as long as it's the cheapest. Pawnshops are also good places for these.

Once you have a game cartridge to get rid of, you need to go to a big department store like K-mart or anything similar. Buy the game that you really want, doesn't matter how expensive it is because you are going to get your money back. You then go home and remove the actual gaming chip or board from its plastic cartridge. You do this with both the one you bought and want to keep and the one that you want to get rid of. Depending on the system, you'll usually only need a pair of pliers to remove the screws and open the case. You switch the games from their outer casing and close them back up again. Now you have the game you want in a cartridge with a different title on it. Make a photocopy of the manual of the game you bought and pack everything back up into the box. Now you bring the expensive game back to the store you bought it from and depending on their policy (read their return policies on electronics before returning anything), you either tell them that you don't like it or that it's defective. If the store you went to only lets you exchange it for another game, that isn't a problem. Because you can then bring that one back the day after, unopened and they'll give you your money back. It always works and you can get a great library of games at very little cost.

CASTING JOBS

This is a nice way to make some easy money on the side. It mainly involves working in films or television as a background (extra) person. Average pay is around ten to twenty dollars and you're usually guaranteed a certain amount of pay, even if you only work for one hour. They normally feed you snacks and if you're there for a certain amount of time, you'll get lunch too. You also don't need any special skills to get work. To put your name into these agencies is pretty simple and inexpensive, sometimes free. Of course, this works best if you live in or near a fairly big city. Look in the yellow pages under 'Casting agencies', call them up to see what their criteria is and how much the fee is (if any). Usually you'll need some sort of picture of yourself; preferably a headshot and you'll have to go in to fill out a form with your height, hair color, etc.

If you do need to pay a fee you usually won't pay more than twenty or thirty dollars to put your name in and if you want to work a lot you'll need to go to more than one agency. The more agencies that have your name, the better chance you have of working. This is just a way to get some extra money on the side, if you live in a major film haven you can make a living off this but you need to be persistent if you want to work a lot. My advice is to call them every week (unless they tell you otherwise) to see if there is anything going on and don't be afraid to call them.

You can also keep an eye out in the classified ads under 'Auditions' or 'Models', big productions will usually advertise in the paper if they need a lot of people. If there's a movie being filmed or you know of a movie that is coming to your town. Find out the production company that is producing it and you can then call them up and ask which casting agency they are using. You can then go to that casting agency and ask them for work. It's easy money and it's a good job to catch up on your reading or your sleep, depending on which you prefer.

GARBAGE

If you aren't afraid to pick up stuff that was put in the garbage then you won't mind doing this. Good money and good items could be had to whoever is willing to go out and get it. I'm not talking about going through people's garbage looking for crap. I'm talking about going around on garbage day to see if anyone has thrown anything of value in the trash. You can get TV's, freezers, tables, computers, etc. A lot of times people throw stuff out either because they don't need it anymore or have replaced it with something newer. To find out when the trash days are in a particular neighborhood, call the city and ask them. Also, different neighborhoods have different trash. Middle class neighborhoods are the best to look through, as people with houses tend not to pick up each other's garbage so you have a better chance of finding something. Always keep your eye out for stuff and when you see something don't hesitate or else someone will beat you to it. If you want to make money off the stuff you find, the best way is to go to a flea market where it cost you very little to set up and you can get good prices for your items. Some items like a freezer or a ping-pong table could be sold in newspapers. No matter what you sell, always sell it at a reasonable price. You'll move your merchandise and you'll make money.

FREE MOVIES
PART 2

Here are two more little tricks to get your money's worth at the theaters. The first one should be done with someone else or there's no point to it. This way you split the cost on a ticket. Just one person goes to the ticket booth to buy a ticket, about thirty minutes before the movie starts. You need to make sure that you make an impression on whoever is selling your ticket. You can make small talk or ask for the time, or drop your change on the floor. Once you have your ticket you go walk around for twenty minutes or so. Ten minutes before the show starts, you give your ticket to your friend and go back to the theater at the ticket booth to the same person who sold you your ticket. You tell them you bought your ticket some half hour before and that you can't find it. Make sure he or she remembers you and they'll let you in. Your friend in the mean time comes in with the ticket you bought in the beginning. Obviously don't go to the same theater if you plan on doing this often.

Another little trick is this very simple one. Smaller theaters usually check your ticket as you are going into the cinema and let you roam free once you're inside. So there is no one that actually checks your ticket at the door of each movie entrance. You can then go see a movie and when the movie is finished you go to the washroom until the next movie you want to see starts. You then go to the next movie and you can keep doing this all day long. Very simple but you can get a whole day's worth of entertainment for the price of one movie. Even cheaper if you use the above system and go with a friend.

SUMMER CAMPS

This trick will give you one or all of the following, a free place to stay for a while, food, a lot of free stuff and/or money. I'll start off first by describing what this system is and then I'll follow up with the tools necessary and on how to go about finding these camps.

There are a lot of seasonal camps all over North America and I'm sure all over the world. The best camps to go to are the summer camps, which are in operation only during the summer months and close down sometime in the fall. That means you can go there in the wintertime and it'll be deserted and you'll have free run of the place.

You'll need a few essential tools if you plan on doing this properly. A word of advice, get quality tools. The worst is to have your screwdriver bend before you can get the window open, quality will mean all the difference. Most important is a strong flat head screwdriver or a set of mechanic pry bars. Lock cutter pliers are extremely useful but a little big to carry. Two vice grips, which are used to twist chain links so as to remove any chains, which might get in your way. You'll also need a hammer to help knock off any locks and to assist your screwdriver in the opening of entrances. Carry everything in a good, sturdy shoulder bag that lets you get in and out hassle free.

To find which summer camps might be in your area, just look in the yellow pages under 'Summer Camps'. You then proceed to contacting them and asking for any available information they have on their camp and during what time of year they are open, as some summer camps are open during the winter and cater to the outdoor crowd. Another good way to get lots of information on these camps is to look in the newspapers and exhibition halls around springtime. Around this time all the camps get together and try to get people interested in their programs. If you live in a big city these are common and make the footwork a lot easier and faster to complete because you can just go there and pick up a bunch of pamphlets. You can then use the summer time to do your research and then hit them in the fall. It's good to scope out any camps you want to visit well in advance to get familiar with them and the territory.

Now comes the time for you to pay a visit to the camp and perhaps make some money in the long run. You should have as much room available in your vehicle as possible so take out anything which you won't need. The more room you have, the more stuff you can take. You need to be as discreet as possible when going there so I recommend going late at night so you'll have better cover. Most of these places are out in the countryside with very few houses (if any) around so it makes them ideal to go to.

When you arrive at the camp make sure there is no one around. Look for any vehicles parked nearby. If someone is there and does spot you, you can simply say you are lost and that you are looking for directions. If the coast is clear, locate the largest building; this is usually the main house where the kitchen is located along with washrooms and usually some beds. This is an ideal place to settle in for the night and to setup as your base. The easiest way to get into any of these buildings is through the window. One thing to do before you try to break into any building is to check all doors and windows to see if they are locked, you'd be surprised sometimes. To get in through the windows you use either a flat head screwdriver or a pry-bar (not a crow-bar). You insert it in where you see the latch that keeps the windows locked and you just force the window open while using your other hand to help slide it open. Most latches on windows are flimsy and will give with enough pressure from a pry-bar. Once you're in you can close the window again and just use the door. If someone comes you can tell them you were lost and came to find help. It was late and no one was there and the door was open so you thought you would stay the night and leave in the morning.

Camps usually shut everything down during the off-season. This includes electricity and water. They usually turn off all the switches in the fuse box so generally you just need to locate this and turn them on. I recommend not using any lights at night other than your flashlight. Sometimes the breaker/fuse box will be in a little shack somewhere near the main house. The same goes for the water situation, usually it's in its own little shack and everything needs to be turned on including the water pumps. So if you want water, you'll need electricity.

When the morning comes you can then scope out the rest of the grounds to see what there is to take. You'll find canoes, kayaks, tents, radios, ATV's and so on, located throughout all the camps' buildings. Only start collecting stuff when you are ready to leave (in the event of someone coming over, you don't want to have a bunch of stuff piled beside your car) and if you went to the camp with that single purpose then I suggest doing this at the first light of day and getting out right after.

Start by looking for the keys to all the houses. If the keys are on the premises they will usually be kept in the main house somewhere or in the tool or utility shed. This way you won't have to break into any other building. Before you take anything, take a look around and see what you want and what you can take. When you know what you want you can then pack up the car fast and can be out in a very short while. Remember, any building or shed or box that is locked can usually be opened with a strong screwdriver or pry bar. Either the latch or the wood will give way and this is the only tool you should need to get into any place.

As I mentioned before, you'll find sports equipment, backpacks, if there's a lake nearby you'll find canoes or kayaks. You can also get fridges and stoves if that's your cup of tea. Usually there will be canned foods, which you can also take or eat while you're there. An ATV or two can usually be found too which they use for work.

You will obviously need a pick up or trailer if you want to take an ATV. If you can't find the keys for the ATV you can take it home and remove the ignition and replace it by a simple on/off switch, which you can get a Radio Shack. You can either leave with everything in your car or you can bring everything out in the woods on the camps property, near a public road and hide it there. This way you can leave the premises with an empty car and go pick it up when you're ready. When you're home you can sell everything and make some very good money. Once you leave the camp grounds do not go back for any reason, especially if you are taking anything. You never go back to the scene of the crime and that's very important to remember. So make sure you get everything you want from it the first time you are there.

Alternatively, you can use these camps just as lodgings and enjoy a vacation away from the city in the quietness of the wilderness. The best camps are the ones far away from a city or town where there won't be anyone around and where there won't be any cops. The more remote it is, the longer you can stay there without anyone noticing you are there. I prefer doing this in the late fall before the snow covers the ground, it just makes it easier to get around. And these places have insurance so you needn't worry about taking things from the kids. If anything, you are doing the kids a favor because when they come back next summer they'll have new equipment from the insurance. Enjoy this and do your research, it pays well in the end.

MAIL

This is a good trick to get some credit card numbers, social security numbers, checks or anything similar. You get these by delivering junk mail to mail boxes and taking what's inside. You can get a job like this by looking in the classified ads for companies, which are hiring couriers to pass out flyers/junk mail. There is usually always someone hiring because the turnover for these companies is quite high. Most companies hire on the spot and don't do any interviews. They'll give you a bag similar to a postman's, along with that you'll get a bunch of flyers, which you'll need to deliver. When you get to a mailbox and there's no one around, you place your flyer in it and take whatever is in there and place it in your bag. Make sure no one is watching when you do this. When you have had enough just go home with the bag. The employer won't think much of it, as this is a frequent thing for people to do if they don't like the job. When you're in the comfort of your own home you can proceed to take a look at your loot. SSN's, bank account numbers, checks, credit cards, and other personal information can all be used with other scams in this book.

FED-EX INSURANCE

This is a simple thing to do. It involves sending something across town or country and claiming that it was damaged when the other party received it. In return, you'll get refunded for the amount you insured the item for.

What you'll need for this is a receipt of the item you are sending and a place to send it to. The location part is simple. You can either go to a Fed-Ex drop location and ship it to yourself at your home address or you can choose to send it to a friend. As for the receipt, I strongly advise that you have a receipt if you don't want to have a hassle. You can either ship something which no longer works or which you don't want anymore.

You pack the parcel properly and ship it off with insurance. When you receive the package, take it in and say nothing to the driver. I advise that you now drop the parcel from a good height of three feet or so. Make sure that if you are shipping something you don't want any more that it no longer works after you receive it. Call them up thirty minutes later and complain that your radio, computer or whatever no longer works and that it looks like the box was dropped. They'll send someone over to investigate, normally the guy will just come over to make sure that the item no longer works and to check to see if there was any damage done to the outside of the box. Within a few weeks you'll get a check for the value of your item.

FREE PAYPHONES

This is an old trick and it's very, very simple. All you do is call the operator and tell him or her that you just tried to make a phone call but the payphone took your money. The operator will ask you what number you were trying to call and they'll place the call for you. It's a very simple way to make a call if you don't have any change.

VIDEO STORES

This will get you free movies and video games, which you'll be able to keep. All you have to do is become a member at a video store and give them a fake address and fake number. Some video stores will ask for proof of residence. In which case you can keep a utility bill from your previous address or you can go to the DMV and change your address on your driver's license to a fake one. You can also scan a utility bill in your computer, alter the address and print it out. You then proceed to rent as many movies and/or video games as you are allowed and you never show up at the video store again.

Video stores won't try much harder to reclaim their merchandise past making a few phone calls to the fake number you gave them. There are so many video stores out there that you can have quite a collection. Another way is to hang around the counter pretending to be looking at whatever might be near and listening to people as they rent movies. A lot of store (outside of Blockbuster) will let you rent without your membership card or any ID. They just require the phone number and the name of the account. Listen in and make note when someone gives out his or her number and name. You can then proceed to rent under their name on a different occasion. I recommend going online or looking in the phone book for the address of that person. A good place online for that is www.411.com or www.411.ca. This way you'll have a little extra information in case you are asked for it.

If you want to make money off this, you can rent console games and sell them to friends or on eBay or anywhere you can.

COURIER FLIGHTS

This is not anything illegal nor is it extraordinary but a lot of people don't know about this little trick and it's a great way to get cheap flights. Everyday, international courier companies send tons of documents between countries. Because of certain restrictions, these packages cannot travel as passenger baggage unless there is a passenger accompanying it to clear it through customs. In the past, couriers were able to travel for free but in recent years these companies saw that this was a good way to make some extra revenue so they started charging a fee. They call it 'an administration fee' but it's obvious that they're just trying to make money. Average cost for return flights is usually a couple of hundred dollars for overseas and less for flights to South America. But you need to have an open schedule and be ready to leave whenever a flight becomes available. It's rare where you'll be able to choose the day and time when you want to leave.

Most flights are return and last anywhere from a day to a few weeks. Prices tend to vary according to the time of year just like regular flights. November and February are the cheapest and Christmas and summer are the most expensive. Some companies will give you a lower price the more flights you take with them. It's a lot harder to get domestic flights within the U.S. then it is to get international flights. If you want to know what flights are available you can write to them asking for their flights and prices (include a self-addressed stamped envelope). You can also look them up in the yellow pages or on the Internet (under 'International Couriers') and call them up directly. It helps if you live near or in a city, which has a big airport, as most of these companies tend to be located in the close proximity of airports. You can also find flights back to North America from overseas by simply looking in the phone book. Best to be in a major city in Europe or else you won't be going very far. Most companies charge a membership fee of forty to fifty dollars to get registered with them. From there you will just be paying the cost of the flight ticket.

FREE CREDIT REPORTS

Here's an easy way to get your credit report and an easy way to a quick fix for it. If you have any negative feedback in your credit history then you are going to have a hard time getting credit anywhere. To get your credit report, apply for a credit card at a bank. If you aren't accepted they'll send you a letter telling you so along with the name of the credit bureau they used. If it's not listed, call your bank and ask them what agency they deal with and the address of the agency. You have thirty days from the time you received the letter from the bank to ask the credit bureau for your credit report. Send them a letter requesting your report along with a copy of the rejection letter from the bank. This will cost you nothing at all as long as you write to them within thirty days of rejection. Once you receive your report, you can then write back to the agency asking them to review your file, by doing this, it will wipe off some of the negative information you might have. The way it works is that the agency will write to each of the companies that made a complaint about you, asking them to verify the information. The companies in turn will have a limited number of days to reply, if they do not reply, that complaint will be taking off your report. By doing this, you have very good chances of clearing your entire report.

RENTING

This one has to do with renting video, audio and sports equipment. You can use your own name or someone else's if you have it. I'll start off by talking about video and audio. There's a lot of places out there that rent or lease DVD players, TV's, and stereos by the month with a lot of places doing an almost nil credit check because they are so desperate to rent it out to you. Let's say you wanted to rent a DVD player, you could then call a place like Rent-a-Vision, which is quite easy to get things from, and inquire about renting a player. Ask about different models and get one that is on the high end of the scale. The beauty with this is that you never need to go into the store. They can do it all by telephone. They'll call you back after a few hours after they've done the paperwork to let you know if you are accepted or not. If they check your credit and you have a really bad credit history they might ask you to put a deposit down for the partial sum of the item. They'll take down your bank information and your employment. Have a friend waiting at his home for the phone call and have him pose as your employer. Usually everything is done the same day and you'll also have to make the first payment. A couple of weeks after receiving it, you change your address and phone number. If someone call's your friend looking for you, all he has to say is that he has no idea what they are talking about.

If you are planning on moving then I suggest that you do a whole bunch of them at once. You can look in the yellow pages under 'Rentals' and rent whatever you can get your hands on, pool tables, arcade games, computers, power tools, satellites. Once you take off it won't make a difference. You can also rent a cheap apartment somewhere and set up some empty boxes and blankets and little knick-knacks. It'll look like you are just moving in. Once you get all your stuff you pack up and take off with the goods. If you do this with your own name, you will definitely ruin your credit and if you do this a lot you might have a couple of people looking for you also. So I recommend doing this only if you really need the money or if you have alternate ID. You can make a whole lot of money with this if you do it a lot. And if you are doing this just for the money then be sure you get things you can easily sell. This is a good trick to do when you don't want to displace yourself and you also want to fill your time by doing something profitable.

TELEPHONES

If you have a telephone line connected already and you want to make some quick money then you can get a phone from your telephone service provider and sell it. A lot of phone companies, along with the service they offer, will rent telephones out. You can use this trick to get a telephone (the most expensive one) and then selling it after to make some extra cash. Some telephone providers will give you a calling card also. This you can sell to people and use it for yourself and make as many calls as you want. Your telephone line itself will last a couple of months before the company finally decides to disconnect you for having a high bill and not paying. Now, if you want to do this and keep your telephone line connected.

I recommend doing this trick and calling the company up to tell them that you are moving and no longer need a phone line. Give them a fake address to forward your bill to. When this is done, you can then call the company up a few days after ask them to get a phone line connected where you live. It varies from company to company, most companies will ask for some ID to connect a line. If you give them different ID numbers then last time you shouldn't have a problem connecting a new line. You can also give them your middle name as your first name. Your file number consists of your name along with your ID numbers, which is why you can give them different numbers each time. If you wait 'til the phone line gets disconnected before changing the address, then you might have problems getting a new line in there. They will view your address as a problem for them and require that you pay a deposit to get a new line put in. Make sure you tell them that you have never had a phone line before when you connect a line.

EXCHANCE TRICK
Number Two

This one is pretty obvious but I'd like to include it anyways. This trick lets you replace something that is broken for something new. You can get a new one by simply buying the exact same thing and then bringing back the old one and asking for your money back. The broken item needs to look fairly new though or you can simply take out the part you need out of the new one and bringing it back without saying a word. If you do this in big department stores you shouldn't have any problems at all getting your money back. When you bring something back like this, don't tell them that it's broken, you just tell them that it's not what you want and you just want your money back.

BUYING AND SELLING

A good way to make some money legally is to buy items at a low price and sell them at profit. This is just to give you an idea of how to start going about this. Good places to look for bargain items are in the classified section of newspapers and on online auction sites such as eBay. Look for headings such as 'Wholesale lots' or 'Flea Market/Surplus items'. These will usually be big lots, which you can buy at pretty low prices and then turn around and sell it back on eBay as smaller lots. If you know the value of certain goods like cameras, you can keep an eye out for bargains that are at least sixty percent off its current market value. The best place to go to if you want to make lots of money, are police and municipal auctions. To find out where these and other auctions from different liquidators are located just look in the classified ads for 'Auctions'. Police and municipal auctions are usually held at regular intervals so you can call a police station and inquire about it or call the city to find out when they hold their auctions. These are the auctions you will get the best bargains at since most items are recovered objects that were lost or stolen or just surplus stock. Other auction houses tend to have higher prices because people actually want to make a good profit off the item their selling so it won't sell below a certain price. When going to auctions, always look for things, which you can easily sell. Buying a couple of lampposts for two bucks might be a great deal but if you're stuck with them there's no point.

Tips for selling are as follows. For anything, which is career oriented such as drafting tables, cameras, microscopes and what not. Some good places to sell these are on campus at universities. It's free and there's usually always a student who's looking for equipment. Newspapers work well for the most part, they cost a little bit of money but if you have something, which is popular and will sell fast, it's a good way to go. An odd place perhaps to some, but which works very well would be taverns. All sorts of people hang out in taverns and many are interested in bargains. If you want to sell something this way make sure that you are selling it at a good price or else not many people will be interested. You won't make as much money this way but you'll sell you goods. The best place by far and which is quite cheap is eBay. Thousands upon thousands of people look there everyday for merchandise. And people will buy almost anything there. Set up an account and you're ready to go. They charge you a small percentage of the selling price plus a small insertion fee for placing the auction. Anything that you are interested in selling I recommend that you look it up online to get the current value of it. This way, you'll know what it goes for and you'll be able to ask for a price that will be attractive to the buyer. And one final tip, never sell anything in pawn shops.

One more place, which has brought me much profit, is the local flea market. If you have one near your home you should go check it out to see what sort of things they sell there. These are a great place to set up and sell your wares or goods. You can gather stock for a while and when you have enough you bring everything you have and try your best. With so many people passing through most flea markets, usually you'll find some who's interested in what you have. If you want to sell anything, be it at the flea market or anywhere else, I highly suggest that you check the prices of any stock you have and set a price accordingly. No one is going to buy a ten year old stereo system for a hundred dollars when they can by a brand new one for the same price. That is the biggest mistake that most people make when trying to sell something.

On a final note, I recommend never going to a pawnshop to sell anything. Only go there if you are desperate for pocket money and don't have time to sell through a different format. Pawnshops are in business to make money and if they are going to sell used items, they cannot give you as much as they are able to sell it for. So usually they'll offer an eighth or a tenth of the price it's worth brand new. Unless you suffer from extreme laziness or from an extreme lack of money I recommend staying away from these places.

CEMETARIES

I don't personally find this scam interesting, as there are things that I simply won't do. But having spent a good bit of time in cemeteries and investigating around, I know you can make some decent money. If you are absolutely going to die and you're living on the streets perhaps you might be interested in this. A lot of the bigger cemeteries have mausoleums and most of these are quite old. Being old they are pretty easy to get into if you wanted to. Usually playing around with the lock will open them up or if you'd rather, you can just kick it in or use a crowbar. What you are looking for is not jewelry but skulls. Skulls can fetch a very good price on the market. A lot of pre-med or med students at universities would buy such a piece. A thousand dollars is not unheard of for a skull. If you aren't afraid of spirits coming after and if you are hard put, this might be for you. Another good use for mausoleums is to use them as shelter if you need to. As I mentioned they are easy to get into and if you need a place to stay for a night you can crash in one of them.

NRI AND ICS
SCHOOLS

What these two schools offer are courses by mail, which you pay on a monthly basis. More often than not, depending on the course, they give materials relating to the course also. If you take a computer course, you'll get a computer as you're 'tool'. If you take locksmithing, you'll get everything you need to cast and make keys and open locks. So on and so on. They ship you your equipment after you have completed a certain percentage of the course. So the faster you do it, the faster you'll get the goods and the less you'll have to pay. It takes about three months before you can receive anything and this is if you complete the sections of the course as you get them. It's all very easy as the answers are in the book and it's all open book. You do the exams at home and then send them in.

The way it works is very simple. Write to the school (address or phone number can be found on the internet) and apply to whichever course you want materials from. They'll ask you to send a small deposit of twenty dollars or so and then they will send you the course material. After which you make a payment every month and after you've complete about a third of the course you will receive you're tools. When you receive your initial course pack, wait two weeks or so and call them up saying that you only just received your course material. They will change you due date for your payments. This will give you a couple more weeks, which equals money in your pocket. Do all the course material right away and instead of mailing the answers in, you should phone them in. This gets you your materials faster. I've completed enough of the courses after three months to get my tools. Total cost comes out to about one hundred and twenty dollars (forty dollars a month). Not bad for a brand new computer. When you get your computer or whatever else you are supposed to get. Call the school and change your address and phone number. That's about it, after that you never have to deal with them again and you can either keep or sell what you got.

LOCK PICKS

Lock picks are always useful to have around. Providing you know how to use them of course. They can help you get around and can make some money for you too. I won't try to describe how to use lock picks as there are whole books on the subject and if you are interested I suggest you pick one of them up to learn more about picks. I will just do a run through of some of the different picks available on the market and how you can get your hands on them. And I'll offer a suggestion or two in the end of how you can make money with them.

-The most basic and maybe the most complex, seeing that they require a lot of practice to learn how to use them, are the steel picks and tension wrenches. They have been used throughout history but as I said, they are time consuming to learn.

-Next, we have the padlock picks. These usually come in a set and open most padlocks. They require a lot less time than the tension picks and are relatively cheap to buy.

-Next in line would be sesame decoders. A little practice with them and you should get the hang of them. They're useful when trying to figure out the combination of sesame locks.

-Slim Jims are probably the most used picks in existence right now. There are many different models of Slim Jims, which go for many different models of cars. They're a bit primitive but can work wonders in opening a car door. Usually when you buy a Slim Jim you need to verify what model cars that that specific one opens. These will require some actual practice on a real car.

-Tubular lock picks are good because they open the locks to most vending machines. These are my favorite because they are pretty simple to learn and the payback is quick. Soda machines, washing machines, cigarette and candy dispensers. There are a few models of these; each made to open a specific lock according to the number of pins inside the pick. It is best to have a few of them if you plan on doing anything with them. Cost of these picks is moderately priced, not cheap but affordable nonetheless.

-Lock pick guns are seen in a lot of movies as being the high tech pick which you just need to insert in the lock and pull the trigger. They aren't as simple as that and do require some practice. They are simpler than the tension wrenches and picks and with some practice you'll get the hang of it pretty fast. They are bulkier too which sometimes is not a good thing and they are maybe the most expensive picks so far that I mentioned.

-Last and probably the most high tech are electronic lock picks. They require some practice but once you get a hang of it, they'll open most locks in seconds. They are small which makes them quite concealable and you could carry it wearing just shorts and a t-shirt and no one would know. These are by far, the most expensive of the picks with the average price being in the hundreds of dollars.

Having skimmed briefly the different picks available you now have a better understanding of lock picks and you can proceed to finding one, which suits your needs. There are books written for each of these different types of picks. I suggest buying one of those and then deciding whether you want to spend the money on it or not. Order catalogues from places, which offer picks; most of them have books to sell along with their picks. A good place to look for these is the magazine Soldier of Fortune. Here's some help in buying lock picks. Some places might require you to show them proof that you are in the locksmithing business. A lot of these places will just require you to send them a business card or a letterhead from your business. You can print this up on your computer or go to a printing place and have them print out some sample stationary for you. These requirements are listed usually on the order form in their catalogues, so just find one, which you'll be able to order from.

I'm sure you can think of a dozen different things right now to use lock picks to make money. I mentioned one earlier which was for vending machines. Find machines that are unguarded or unwatched at night such as rest areas or gas stations. Not only do you get money from the machines but you also get the goodies, which are inside. Well, if you choose to go with picks, practice a lot, as the more you practice the faster you'll be able to open locks, which means that you'll be out of there faster. Good luck.

FREE PC GAMES

This is a great way to get almost any retail computer game you want for free. The only requirements, a computer and you need a high speed Internet connection if you want to get anywhere. These days, most people have high-speed connections so that should not be too much of a problem. You can get all the latest games for free along with the old classics. New release games are usually available a couple of weeks after they come out. It's very easy and all you need to know is where to look for them. You can rest assure that if there is a software program of any sort that it will be available for free off the internet.

One very fast and painless way to get them is to use a peer-to-peer file-sharing program. There are a lot of them out there and all of them have the capability to share software, videos, music and so on. Gnutella, Emule, Shareaza, uTorrent and many others. You can download these for free off the Internet, simply do a search for them in a search engine and you'll come up with a bunch of them. Once you have the program installed, you can do a search for the particular game you want and chances are it'll come up with a few sources you will be able to download from. Most games and programs are very reliable through this method, meaning that the games are actually what they claim to be and are very stable.

The other way is to actually find a site that has that particular game or program available for downloading. These sites are mainly run by hackers and the good sites are all underground and tend to change internet addresses often as they get caught and shut down. The only problem with this method is that it takes a little footwork when you first start off. Many people claim to have full version appz and gamez, as they put it but when you try downloading you are filled with pop up ads for porn and the game you want isn't actually available from them. These fake sites open up just to make money off the royalties of the pop up ads that poor, unsuspecting users unleash. Unfortunately, the only way to find out if a site is good or bad is to try downloading a game from them to see if it actually works. Most game sites that offer porn along with their other wares are bogus. True game sites usually don't advertise porn and if they do it's not the main topic. So that's a clue as to what to avoid. When you do find a real site though, the good news is that the links to other sites available from the page are usually good to check out too. The good game sites tend to hang together and to promote each other, which is a good thing. Along with games to download, these sites will have movies, music, application programs, serial numbers and a bunch of other stuff to download.

To do a search on the Internet for some sites you can use the following that is in the brackets in the search field ("gamez" +warez +downloads). This will give you the best results and you can shift through the sites from there.

Alternatively, you can go to one of the following sites, which have lists of the top sites, www.zipwarez.com, Piratebay(torrents), Kickass.to (torrents)s, www.elitetoplist.com, www.warez.com. These sites will save you time because they have direct links the game sites you want and you'll also have less searching to do. There are of course, many other sites with similar lists and all are pretty much the same. So I've now given you two very excellent ways to get full, retail games for free. Following the above steps, you can now proceed to making money off your work. Look in the next section that follows to know how.

PIRACY

Having followed the last section, you now have your hands on a bunch of games, which you can now sell. You can't sell your pirated games on eBay or any of the other online auctioning sites for the obvious reason that they are pirated games and if you don't tell someone that buys your game that it isn't an original they will make a complaint and you won't last long at that site. The best way is to make 'real' copies with your computer and sell them at the Flee market. But before you can sell them to anybody you need to have at least one main piece of hardware. It's fine to have these games on your computer but if you can't copy them on CD-Rom they are useless so you will need to have a CD-writer/CD-burner. A really good one will run you at about thirty bucks or so and if you plan on selling a lot of games it's a good idea to get a fast one, maybe even two so you can make two copies at once. You'll also need a color printer and blank, clear CD labels along with blank CD's of course. Very helpful also, is a shrink-wrap system, which costs around seventy dollars for a decent one.

For any retail game that is out there, the image on the CD and the CD jacket or sleeve is available for downloading off the Internet. One good site is www.covertarget.com. It allows you to print out a sleeve for the CD case with the original graphics that's on it. And with the blank CD labels you can print out a label, which will look just close to the original CD. Put it all together and you have something that looks like you bought it from a store, shrink wrap it and it'll look like a brand new game along with the bar code on the back of the CD case.

To recap, you download full, retail versions from the Internet and then copy them onto CD. From there you print out labels for your blank CD's along with the jacket sleeve of the CD case. You shrink wrap them and go sell them at the flea market or anywhere else you want to. The best method is to have at least twenty or thirty different games and make several copies of each one. You then set up a table at your flea market and sell them at a third of the price. Most recent retail computer games sell for around fifty dollars a game and you can sell yours for fifteen or twenty. In a good day you can make close to a thousand dollars. It costs very little to start up and all the games are free so most of the money you get is pure profit. You can pay for all your expenses even on a bad day.

You can also do the same with Playstation and Xbox console games. All you have to do is rent them from your local video store and copy them onto another CD. Xbox requires you to have a DVD burner though. From there you can follow the steps above to make them look like a retail version and sell them at the flea market. It's a very easy thing to do and allows you to do it when you want to like most scams in this book

CHEQUES

Here's a simple scam, which can make you some really good money. The way this system goes is as follows: You get a check from someone, deposit it in your bank and then take the money out using your bank card. The only problem with this trick is that if you deposit the checks in a bank account that is in your name, you can get in some trouble with the authorities. I'll explain in detail.

There are two ways to opening a bank account. One way is to have it in your name and the other is to have in a fake name. You can acquire some fake ID's through a source or make them yourself with a computer and then proceed to opening a new bank account. Opening a basic bank account is pretty simple and usually requires very basic identifications. There are whole books on the subject, so I recommend reading one of those. If you have an account in a fake name, there is nothing to link that name with yours so it is quite safe. Of course, you can use your real bank account and your real name if you really need the money and go into hiding afterwards. Once you deposit, let's say, someone's paycheck into your bank account and it comes back to them at some later date as a cancelled check the bank will try to contact you first. They do this so that they can hopefully get their money back from you. They will try to get their money before they contact authorities because it is better for them to get the money from you then to have to go through the courts, which means that they will see very little of that money, if they ever do. Also, if you do this on a grand scale then the bank will suspect foul play right away and alert authorities. But then again, if the account isn't in your name, you don't really care.

The trick to getting peoples checks is to go from door to door delivering flyers, a scam I described earlier in this book. You distribute the flyers after the mail has past and you collect people's mail. You can get quite a few paychecks and other various checks this way. A good time of year to do this is when people are going to be receiving their income tax refunds. During this time of year you can get some pretty big checks. Once you have the checks you shouldn't wait to cash them, as it will only be a matter of time before the person complains that he or she never received their check. Remember that eventually that person will get the check back and everything will be okay on their end. The only people that will be out will be the bank.

You deposit all the checks through the bank machine using your bankcard. This way you avoid any contact with any person and the checks you have which are made out to other people will not be questioned. Most checks deposited this way are rarely verified and if they are it's to check to see if it has been endorsed, which it will be of course.

Just sign the back of it in whoever's name it's made out to and then sign it with your name. Remember to deposit only one check at a time, you'll avoid any suspicion if you do this. It'll normally take up to a week for a check to clear this way. When the check clears you can just withdraw the money from anywhere through a bank machine. The only contact you'll ever have is when you first open your bank account and that's it.

You can make a lot of money this way but depending on whether you used your real name or not should stay low. A tip to avoid any trouble is to make sure that the information the bank has about your address and contact is false. Give an address which is not your own, obviously. And give them fake phone numbers for everything and false name and numbers for the contacts, if they want any. This way, nothing can be linked to you. It's an extremely easy way to make money but it is also extremely illegal.

BUYING AND RETURNING

This trick is really done by 'investing' money and getting a higher return on it afterwards. There's several ways you can go about this, they are as follows. You buy something that is on sale at a big name store, the best I found for this is Best Buy. You make sure it's a substantial saving, if it's something that isn't too expensive, buy it when it's forty or fifty percent off. If it's something a little higher priced, buy it when it's hundred dollars or more off the regular price. All you have to do is wait a couple of weeks after it goes back to its regular price and return it without the receipt. Say you bought it a couple of days ago and you changed your mind about giving it as a gift to so and so. Make sure you didn't open the box or else you might have difficulties. If the box isn't open, they'll give you a store credit for what the item is worth, which will be the full price of it, the price you fictionally paid supposedly just a few days prior. It's a very simple method and I've yet to encounter any problems.

Another trick is to buy it when it's on sale and wait for it to go back to its original price. You then buy it again at its full price and ask the cashier for a second copy of your bill. One would be the original receipt and the second would be a gift receipt. A gift receipt is a regular receipt without the price. Most big stores do this now but make sure they do by calling them and asking first. Most electronic stores (such as best buy) offer an extended warranty for an extra price. You want to get this too when you buy your item at its full price (when it's not on sale). You now have two receipts with the full price, one original and one gift receipt. You bring back the item with the original, full price receipt to where you bought it from. You'll get your cash back and then you proceed to go to another store with the item (which you bought on sale) with the full price gift receipt. Some stores will give you money back, some stores will give you a store credit, which you can get a gift card and use it whenever you want to. Getting cash back with the gift receipt not only depends on the store but also on the person serving you. One week you can get a credit and the next week at the same store with a different person, you might get cash back. This is really worth it when you can buy something that's a few hundred dollars off the original price. So in the end you got the full value back of an item you bought a couple of hundred dollars cheaper. If you end up getting credit back, you can then buy more items on sale and then proceed to repeating the trick again to receive even more credit and/or cash. Also, gift cards are easily sold on Ebay or any other auction sites. This trick is really easy to do if you live in a big town where one of the big chains has a lot of stores, once again such as Best Buy.

You can use the second part of this trick to get a receipt for an item without actually having to pay anything for it. If you already own something or purchased something somewhere else at an extremely low price, you can then use the receipt trick to be able to bring it back at a big store that carries the same thing and get the full value of your merchandise.

BOOK STORE BUYING
AND EXCHANGE

Here's a quick trick concerning bookstores that follows the same lines as the last system. There are a lot of small bookstores out there that sell books or audiotapes at liquidation prices. Check to see if a big chain such as Barnes and Nobles carry the same stock. Most times, you'd be surprise to find out that the same book cost four times as much at a big chain. You buy a few of these cheapies and then you bring them to the big name store. You tell them that you received the items as a gift and don't like them. You say that you would like a store credit. The cashier will then tell you to go find the books you want and he or she will make the exchange for you. You end up paying twenty bucks or so and get back about a hundred dollars worth of brand new books.

You can also ask for gift certificates instead of getting books. Then go back to the store at a later date and buy some books with the gift certificates. Wait a day or two and return the books to the store and ask for your money back and they'll give it to you. The reason for this is that on the receipt it says that you purchased the books with gift certificates, which is as good as real money. It never said that made a return to get the certificates in the first place. About half the time when you get gift certificates this way, the cashier would stamp them 'merchandise only'. They never stamp the receipt for the books this way though, which is why you can get money back for them. You can also do this with books you get from book clubs which cost you absolutely nothing. With a few good choices from certain book clubs you can get about two to three hundred dollars worth of books that you could bring back per membership.

GAMBLING

This is more of a little trick than a scam. There's no con going on here, just a simple trick to help you win if you gamble. My advice is if you can resist, don't gamble in the first place. But if you must, at least you'll know a little something, which can help you even the odds a little bit. This trick can be used with pretty much any gambling game but I find it works great with blackjack or roulette, any game that gives double your money back on a bet.

It works like this: You place a bet of around five bucks and if you lose you double it. Betting ten dollars on the next round, if you lose again you double it again to twenty dollars and so on (five to ten to twenty to forty to eighty, etc). If you win, you place your bet back at five dollars. Example: I place five dollars on black while playing roulette, the ball lands and I lose. My next bet will be ten dollars and I lose again. On my third try I bet twenty dollars and win, my fourth bet will therefore be five dollars. I win on my forth so I keep it at five dollars. I win again and it continues to stay at five. On my sixth bet I lose so I raise my bet to ten and keep proceeding like this for the entire time while I'm gambling. Instead of five dollars as a starting bet, you can bet anything. Starting at one dollar and doubling from a buck works the same way (one to two to four to eight to sixteen, etc).

I'll explain why this is a good system. Every time that you win, let's say with the five bucks starting bet, you'll win five dollars. If you start doubling from one dollar, you'll win a dollar every time you win a hand. You spend five dollars on the first hand and you lose, you then bet ten dollars on the next and lose again. That's fifteen dollars that you lost so far. On the third hand you are now betting twenty dollars and you win. You won twenty and lost fifteen so you made a profit of five dollars. It works like this no matter how high you go. If you start your betting at five dollars, when you do win, your winning bet will always be five dollars more than the total you lost while doubling up. To really get a feel for this try it with pennies in a fictional game or try it in a computer game, it never fails. It takes a while but you're always wining. If you play four hours at roulette, always playing on red or black or playing blackjack and always doubling up from five dollars, you can make a couple of hundred dollars easily.

There are a few drawbacks to this system, it does take a while, you do need patience as your sitting there and just doubling up, especially if you're playing roulette because you have no decisions to make really. And if you are playing roulette, I recommend always keeping it on the same color. The other drawback is that you need to have enough money to cover yourself while you are doubling up. It's good to have enough money to cover losing at least six times in a row, more if you can afford it. If you start on five dollars that means that you'll need three hundred plus dollars. If you start on one dollar, you'll only sixty dollars or so. The more money you have the better off you'll be. The starting bet tells you how much you'll be winning on the hands you do win. If you start with two dollars and start doubling from there, you'll win two bucks every time you have a winning hand.

If you really want to make some money, you can bring a friend along to help you out. You need two people to do this next trick. It uses the system I just described but it lets you win on every round. You need to play the roulette to utilize this trick also. You decide what amount you want to start with. If you don't have a lot of money I recommend starting with a dollar. Also it's good to start small to get a hang of it. You place your bets on red and black. So your buddy places a dollar on black and you place a buck on red. Whoever loses doubles his bet and whoever wins bets a buck. It's the same system as before, each person takes care of his own betting and when one loses, he doubles and when one wins, he places his bet back at a dollar. What happens here is that as a team, you are always winning a dollar whenever the ball lands because it has to land on either red or black. The only thing that can happen to make both people lose is if the ball lands on zero or double zero in which case, you both would double up and continue with the system.

Example: Tim bets a buck on red and Jim bets a buck on black. The ball lands on red so Tim keeps his bet at a buck and Jim doubles his to two dollars. Ball lands on red again so Tim bets a buck and has now won two dollars, Jim doubles up to four dollars and has lost three dollars (one buck the first round and two on the second). Ball lands on black this time so Tim doubles to two bucks and Jim wins four dollars (for a profit of one dollar) and bets one dollar. You see that whenever the ball lands the duo has made a dollar and if it lands on one of the two zeros then they simply didn't win a dollar on that round but will continue to do so after that. Once again, try it with pennies or on a computer game to really see it in action. Practice it a while before you go out, this way you'll be more comfortable with it.

DIRECTORY

'Bill me' clubs:

Bradford Exchange-Plates
40 Pacific CRT
P.O. Box 5290,
London, Ontario,
N6X 5T5, Canada

9345 Milwaukee Ave.
Niles, Illinois,
60714-9960, USA

Franklin Mint-Misc. Collectibles
1-800-THE-MINT
Canada and USA

Hamilton Collection-Collectibles
4810 Executive Park Ct,
P.O. Box 44051,
Jacksonville, Florida,
32231-4051, USA

Ashton-Drake Galleries-Dolls
40 Pacific Court,
London, Ontario,
N5V 3K4, Canada,
1-800-524-0524

Movie/Entertainment Book Club-Books
33 Oakland Ave.,
Harrison, New York,
10528, USA

Newbridge Book Clubs-Books
3000 Cindel Drive,
Delran, New Jersey,
08370, USA
1-609-786-9778
And includes the following clubs-
        -Architect's and Designer's Book Club
        -Astronomy Book Club

       -Behavioral Science Book Club
       -Early Learning Book Club
       -Executive Program
       -Garden Book Club
       -Instructor's Book Club
       -Intermediate Book Club
       -Library of Computer and Information Sciences
       -Library of Science
       -Library of Speech and Language
       -Mac Professional's Book Club
       -Middle School Book Club
       -Natural Science Book Club
       -Newbridge Multimedia Club (CD-ROMs)
       -Nurse's Book Society
       -PC User's Book Club
       -Reader's Subscription
       -Small Computer Book Club
       -Teacher's Book Club
Lenox-Collectibles
1 Lenox Center,
P.O. Box 3022,
Langhorne, Pennsylvania,
19092-9926, USA

Odyssey Books-Used Books
P.O. Box 24028,
London, Ontario,
N6H 5C4, Canada

Nightingale Conant-Audio Programs
1-800-525-9000
US and Canada

Grollier Limited-Books, Some Collectibles
12 Banigan Drive,
Toronto, Ontario,
M4H 1A6, Canada

Readers Digest-Books
Readers Digest Road
Pleasantville, New York,
10570-7000, USA
800-846-2100

Yves Rocher-Cosmetics
P.O. Box 2860,
Champlain, New York,
12919-2866, USA
888-909-0771
Danbury Mint-Collectibles
47 Richards Ave.,
Norwalk, Connecticut,
06857, USA,
800-243-4664

Time Life-Music, Videos, Books
800-950-7887
Canada and USA

Merck and Company-Specialized Books

55 Horner Ave.
Toronto, Ontario,
M8Z 4X5, Canada
415-255-4491
800-387-7278

Doubleday Book Club-Books
Doubledaybookclub.com

Columbia house-Books, CD-ROMS, Audio books, Videos, Music
http://columbiahouse.com
http://columbiahousecanada.com

Mystery Guild-Books
www.mysteryguild.com
www.mysteryguild.ca

Book of the Month Club,
Quality Paperback Book Club,
History Book Club-Books

6550 East 30th street,
P.O. Box 6300,
Indianapolis, Indiana,
42606-6300
www.qpb.com,
www.bomc.com,
www.historybookclub.com,

Military Book Club-Books
www.militarybookclub.com

Along with these clubs there are countless others, including,

Outdoorsman's Edge,
Stage and Screen,
One spirit,
Country Home and Garden,
Good Cook,
Crafter's Choice,
Disney Movie Club.

You can find all these clubs along with other book, video, music clubs at the following web sites. These two sites have links to almost any club you can think of.

http://bookclubdeals.com and
www.booksonline.com
OTHER CONTACTS
Useful addresses and items of interest

Steve Arnold's Gun Room-Lock picks, underground books
P.O. Box 68, Dept I,
Dexter, Oregon,
97431, USA,
541-726-6360,
www.gun-room.com

Paladin Press-Underground books
Gunbarrel Tech Center,

7077 Winchester Circle,
Boulder, Colorado,
80301, USA
303-443-7250
www.paladin-press.com

Eden Press-Underground books
P.O. Box 8410,
Fountain Valley, California,
92728, USA,
800-338-8484
www.edenpress.com

Fs Book Company-Underground Books
P.O. Box 417457, Dept. N
Sacramento, California,
95841-7457, USA916-577-1226
www.fsbookco.com

NEXT DAY ID-Fake ID's
LSL Issuing dep. INT,
P.O. Box 24600, London,
E9 5UZ, UK
www.fakeiduk.com

MAILBOXES ETC-Mail Receiving Service
www.mbe.com
You can locate any store around the world from their website. Now part of
UPS.

RECOMMENDED READING

Reborn In USA: Personal Privacy Though A New Identity
By Trent Sands
Shows you how to build a new identity for protection, privacy or for any other purpose.
Also Available by Trent Sands are Reborn in Canada, and Reborn Overseas

Credit: The Cutting Edge
By Scott French
Describes the in and out's of the credit system along with tips on improving your own credit.

Catch Me If You Can
By Frank W. Abagnale
A book now made into a movie about the true exploits of one of the most innovative con men. Abagnale retells his tale of how and why chose to do what he did. It's a most entertaining book from a most daring criminal.

The Art of the Steal
By Frank W. Abagnale
Explains the tricks of the trade with ways to protect yourself and your assets.

Complete Guide to Lock Picking
By Eddie the Wire
A how-to guide on lock picking your way in and out of places.

Privacy: How to Get It, How to Enjoy It.
By Bill Kaysing
How to stay out of the eyes of people and protecting yourself.

Methods of Disguise
By John Sample
Helpful book on how you can change your mannerisms and looks so that you can fool people some of the people some of the time.

www.ingramcontent.com/pod-product-compliance
Lightning Source LLC
Chambersburg PA
CBHW070816280326
41934CB00012B/3197